best
easy
day hikes

Sedona

D0197856

Help Us Keep This Guide Up to Date

Every effort has been made by the authors and editors to make this guide as accurate and useful as possible. However, many things can change after a guide is published—trails are rerouted, regulations change, techniques evolve, facilities come under new management, etc.

We would love to hear from you concerning your experiences with this guide and how you feel it could be improved and kept up to date. While we may not be able to respond to all comments and suggestions, we'll take them to heart and we'll also make certain to share them with the authors. Please send your comments and suggestions to the following address:

The Globe Pequot Press
Reader Response/Editorial Department
P.O. Box 480
Guilford, CT 06437

Or you may e-mail us at:

editorial@GlobePequot.com

Thanks for your input, and happy travels!

A **FALCON** GUIDE®

Best Easy Day Hikes Series

best
easy
day hikes
Sedona

Bruce Grubbs

FALCON GUIDE®

GUILFORD, CONNECTICUT
HELENA, MONTANA

AN IMPRINT OF THE GLOBE PEQUOT PRESS

⋀**FALCON**GUIDE®

Cover photo and maps: Bruce Grubbs

ISSN: 1537-2901
ISBN-13: 978-0-7627-2216-7
ISBN-10: 0-7627-2216-9

Manufactured in the United States of America
First Edition/Fourth Printing

To buy books in quantity for corporate use
or incentives, call **(800) 962–0973, ext. 4551,**
or e-mail **premiums@GlobePequot.com.**

Acknowledgments

I would like to thank my many hiking companions down the years, who've put up with my incessant trail mapping and photography. Thanks to Duart Martin, my favorite companion on the trail, for abetting yet another book. And finally, thanks to my editors at The Globe Pequot Press, Hrissi Haldezos and Jeff Serena, for making a book out of my rough manuscript.

Contents

Map Legend

Interstate	(15)	State/National Park/National Monument Boundary	
U.S. Highway	(66) (134)		
State or County Road	(47) (190)	Indian Reservation Boundary	— — —
Forest Road	4165	Bridge	⌣
Interstate Highway	⟹	Pass/Saddle	)(
Paved Road	⟹	Cabins/Buildings	■
Gravel Road	⟹	Mine	⚒
Unimproved Road	===⟹	Gate	•—•
Trailhead/Parking	◯ (P)	City/City Grid	◯ ▦
Main Trail	～ ･ ‑	Overlook or Point of Interest	▣
Secondary Trail	⌇ ‑ ‑	Campground	▲
Cross-Country Trail	⋯⋯	Peak/Elevation	
River/Creek/Falls	～⫽		9,782 ft.
Intermittent Stream	‑･‑		✕
Lake	▰	Cliffs	⏖⏖
Spring	⌀‑		N
Marsh	⚶ ⚶	Map Orientation	▲
Forest/Wilderness Boundary	— — —	Scale	0 0.5 1
			Miles

Overview Map

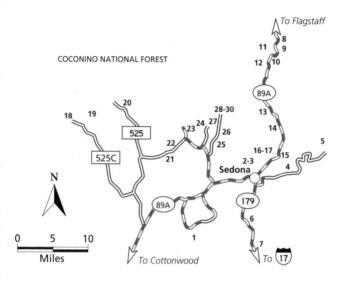

Ranking the Hikes

Although all the hikes in this book are relatively easy, some are longer and have more elevation change than others. To help you pick the type of hike you want, the at-a-glance information at the beginning of each hike includes a short description, the location from Sedona, the type of trail (loop or out-and-back), the difficulty (easy or moderate), the total distance in miles, the high point of the hike in feet, the approximate elevation change, the time required for an average hiker, water sources, the best season, maps, information permits and restrictions (if any), a contact number for additional information, and instructions for finding the trailhead. And to further help you decide, here's a list of all the hikes in order of difficulty.

Introduction

This pocket-sized book contains a selection of the easiest day hikes from my more comprehensive FalconGuide, *Hiking Northern Arizona*. My intention is that this book serve as a low-cost introduction to day hiking in the spectacular Red Rock Country surrounding Sedona, Arizona, for those of you who have limited time or prefer easier hikes. Nevertheless, these hikes provide a generous sample of the great hiking you will enjoy in north-central Arizona. The thirty hikes described here range from 0.5 to 10.0 miles in length; most are just a few miles long and have gentle gradients and a modest elevation change. A few of the hikes are classed as moderate, mainly because of their length. All of the hikes are on established, easy-to-follow trails or follow obvious routes.

Maps

The hikes in this book are easy to follow, and a map shows each trail, so you won't need to buy extra maps. On the other hand, more detailed maps are essential if you decide to explore farther or off-trail. All of the hikes in this book are covered by the detailed topographic maps published by the U.S. Geological Survey, available at local outdoor shops or from the Survey at U.S.G.S. Information Services, Box 25286, Denver, CO 80225; (800) HELP MAP; mapping.usgs.gov. The entire area is also covered by the Coconino National Forest map, available from the Sedona Ranger Station and from bookstores and outdoor shops. This map shows the forest-road network and can be useful for finding trailheads and for general orientation. Another map option for those with a computer is the excellent CD-ROM–based coverage of the Sedona area (Topo! Phoenix and Flagstaff), carried by REI (1–800–426–4840 or www.rei.com). Remember that although topographic maps show the terrain and other natural features very accurately, they are not updated very often. Many of the trails in this book are not shown correctly, or at all, on the topo maps.

Zero Impact

The Red Rock Country is fragile, despite its rugged appearance. Damage done by humans takes many dozens, or even hundreds, of years to disappear. Soils in this high-desert region are thin and easily eroded. Evidence of ignorant and careless recreational use are all too evident along forest roads in the form of litter, trampled vegetation, and massive fire rings. Fortunately, backcountry users are generally better informed and more conscientious than vehicle-based recreationists. Most trail sides reflect this care. A few simple guidelines will help you leave the land and the trail as you found it.

Waste

Pack out all garbage and trash. If you can carry it in full, you can carry it out empty. After your hike dispose of trash at trailhead receptacles, if available, or at a campground, rest area, or other facility. Do not feed wild animals; human food is very bad for them, and animals that become used to human handouts lose their fear of humans and become nuisances that may have to be destroyed.

Human waste must be disposed of carefully or it becomes a health hazard. Select a site at least 100 yards from streams, lakes, springs, and dry washes. Avoid barren, sandy soil, if possible. Next, dig a small "cat-hole" about 6 inches down into the organic layer of the soil. (Some people carry a small plastic trowel for this purpose.)

When finished, refill the hole, making the site as natural as possible. Land managers now recommend that all toilet paper be carried out. Use double zipper bags, with a small amount of baking soda to absorb odor.

Stay on the Trail

Don't cut switchbacks or take other shortcuts. This practice erodes trails, increases the cost of trail maintenance, and costs you more energy than staying on the trail. The ground in many areas is fragile. Soil takes a long time to form in meadows and pinyon-juniper forest, and plants have a tenuous foothold. Avoid walking off-trail in such areas if possible. When traveling cross-country, stay on pine needles, rock, sand, or gravel as much as you can, and spread your group out to avoid creating a new trail. Never blaze trees, construct rock cairns, or build anything else.

Archaeological Sites

The Sinagua (Spanish for "without water") people occupied the Sedona region approximately 1,000 years ago, and many of their ruins and artifacts are scattered throughout the area. Fine examples are preserved at Tuzigoot and Montezuma Castle National Monuments in the Verde Valley. The first European explorers were Spanish Conquistadors under the command of Coronado, who passed through the area in the 1540s. Ruins and artifacts, both pre-Columbian and from the European settlement period, are common in the area. Please treat all ruins and artifacts with respect, no matter where you find them. Stay off walls and structures, and leave all artifacts in place. Many ruins in the area have yet to be studied by archaeologists. A great deal of information can be gained by studying tools, potsherds, chipping sites, and other remains in their original context. If such artifacts are moved or disturbed, an important part of the puzzle is destroyed forever. Pictographs and petroglyphs (rock art) are especially fragile. Such rock drawings and carvings have survived hundreds or thousands of years because the climate is relatively dry. Resist the urge to touch any rock art, as skin oils can quickly degrade the pigments used in rock paintings.

The best way to enjoy ancient ruins and artifacts is from a distance. Take nothing but photographs. Both prehistoric and historic ruins and artifacts are protected by the federal Antiquities Act. If you observe anyone illegally excavating or disturbing a site, please report them to the Sedona Ranger Station at the phone number in the hike description.

Three Falcon Zero-Impact Principles
- *Leave with everything you brought.*
- *Leave no sign of your visit.*
- *Leave the landscape as you found it.*

Play It Safe

Although some of the trails in this book are very near urban areas, others are more remote. In any case you should be prepared for the weather and trail conditions you may encounter. These hikes range in elevation from 3,800 to 7,200 feet. If you normally reside at low elevations, take it easy in the thin mountain air until your body has time to acclimatize, a process that takes several days.

Water and Heat

Although elevations are high, summer days can be hot and dry. Dehydration begins slowly, and its effects are insidious. Prolonged dehydration leads to heat exhaustion and eventually to sunstroke, a life-threatening medical emergency. Long before that point, thirst and dehydration will take the fun out of your hike. Always carry at least a quart of water per person. During the summer months and on the longer hikes, you may need two or more quarts per person. Don't count on finding water on any hike. If you do use natural water sources, remember that all water should be purified before use with a water purifier or iodine tablets. It's easier and safer to carry all the water you'll need from home or town. During the hottest months plan your hike for the early-morning or late-evening hours, or hike one of the canyon trails with water and shade.

Sun

The sun is intense here because of the southerly latitude and high elevations. Wear sun-protective clothing and especially a sun hat. Use a sunscreen lotion with a sun-protection factor of at least 30 for maximum protection against sunburn and the aging effects of sunlight. A tan does not make you immune to sunburn!

Cold

During the summer rainy season (July through mid-September), thundershowers can lower the temperature from the dry and hot nineties to the wet and chilling forties (Fahrenheit) in a matter of minutes. Carry rain gear and an extra layer of warmth, such as a polyester fleece top. Avoid cotton, which loses all its insulating value when wet. Spring and fall weather is almost always delightful during the day, but the nights are cold, with the temperature often dipping near freezing. Be prepared with windproof outer layers and warm gloves and a hat.

Dogs

Dogs are allowed on all the trails in this book, but city ordinances require that they must be on a leash within city limits. In the national forest you must keep your dog under control, either by leash or by voice command. If your dog barks, runs up to other hikers, or chases wildlife, then it is not under control and should be left at home.

Road and Trail Conditions

Most of the trails and their access roads are open year-round. A few trails are reached via dirt roads, which may be very muddy after a winter storm or a heavy summer thunderstorm. The Forest Service sometimes temporarily closes dirt roads until they dry out, to prevent costly road damage. Check with the Sedona Ranger Station, listed in the hike description, for the latest conditions.

Flash floods occur when a sudden heavy rain dumps a large quantity of water into a small area. This can occur during the summer thunderstorm season or during the winter when a warm storm drops rain onto snow covering the headwaters of the canyon. Normally dry washes and drainages can fill with water in a matter of seconds and with no warning. Stay out of narrow canyons during thunderstorm weather. Never attempt to drive across a flooded wash. The roadbed may be washed out, and the depth may be greater than you think. Less than a foot of swift-moving water can wash your vehicle away.

Hike Plan

The Coconino and Yavapai County Sheriffs (911) are responsible for search and rescue in this area. Always tell a reliable person of your hike plans, especially in the remoter areas. On the hike, stick to your plan, and, afterward, be sure to check out with that same person. Rescue teams get a bit irritated when they discover the person they've been looking for all night has been asleep in bed all that time.

Cellular Phones

Cellular phone coverage is generally good in the Sedona area, but coverage is spotty or nonexistent in the remoter areas and canyons. Don't let a cell phone replace common sense and preparedness. Carry appropriate water, food, and clothing for the expected conditions. Backcountry rescue takes hours to organize, and consider that you will probably spend the night out before rescuers can reach you.

Gear Every Hiker Should Carry

- Water
- Food
- Sun hat
- Sunscreen
- Sunglasses
- Durable hiking shoes or boots
- Synthetic fleece jacket or pullover
- Rain gear
- Map
- Compass
- First-aid kit
- Signal mirror
- Toilet paper and zippered plastic bags

Camping

There are several Forest Service campgrounds in Oak Creek Canyon. These include Pine Flat, Cave Spring, Bootlegger, Banjo Bill, and Mazanita Campgrounds. Other public campgrounds in the national forests and state parks in the region are described in *Camping Arizona,* also by Falcon Publishing. Please note that Oak Creek Canyon and the Red Rock Country surrounding Sedona in the Coconino National Forest are closed to vehicle camping except in Forest Service campgrounds.

Access and Services

Sedona can be reached from the south via Interstate 17 and Arizona 179, from the north via Arizona 89A, from the east via Arizona 260, Interstate 17, and Arizona 179, and from the west via Arizona 89A. Shuttle service is available from Phoenix's Sky Harbor Airport. All services are available in Sedona. Motel rooms fill up quickly during holidays and summer, so you may want to make reservations.

SEDONA

1
EAGLES NEST TRAIL

Description: A day hike along Oak Creek in Red Rock State Park.
Location: 5.0 miles southwest of Sedona.
Type of trail: Loop.
Difficulty: Easy.
Total distance: 2.0 miles.
High point: 4,010 feet.
Elevation change: 120 feet.
Time required: 1 hour.
Water: Visitor center.
Best season: All year.
Maps: Sedona USGS quad; Red Rock State Park brochure.
Permits and restrictions: None.
For more information: Red Rock State Park; (928) 282–6907.

Finding the trailhead: From Sedona go west on Arizona 89A to the lower Red Rock Loop Road, which is signed for Red Rock State Park. Turn left and continue 2.9 miles,

Eagles Nest Trail

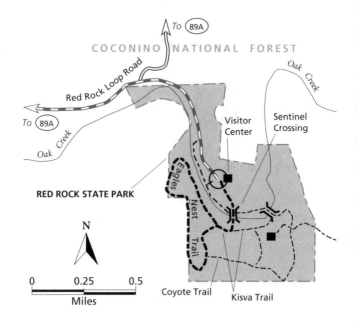

and then turn right on the Red Rock State Park road. Continue past the entrance station to the end of the road at the visitor center.

Key points:
0.0 Visitor Center Trailhead.
0.1 Sentinel Crossing.
0.2 Eagles Nest Trail.

1.8 Kisva Trail.
2.0 Visitor Center Trailhead.

The hike: Red Rock State Park is one of the newest additions to the state park system. In 1986 the state purchased the Smoke Trail Ranch. The ranch was the vacation retreat of Jack Fry, the president of Trans World Airlines. Purposes of the park include the preservation of the riparian habitat of Oak Creek and environmental education. A number of short hiking trails have been built along Oak Creek and on the red sandstone bluffs overlooking the creek.

From the visitor center follow the main trail downhill toward Oak Creek. Turn right at a junction, and cross Oak Creek on a low bridge at Sentinel Crossing. Notice the flood debris piled up from the huge flood that roared down the creek in the winter of 1993. On the far side of the creek, turn right (west) on the Kisva Trail. Continue a short distance, and then turn left (south) on the signed Eagles Nest Trail. This trail crosses an irrigation ditch and then climbs away from the creek via several short switchbacks. At the junction with the Coyote Ridge Trail, turn right (south). The Eagles Nest Trail eventually turns northwest and works its way onto a ridge with a fine view of Oak Creek in the foreground and Cathedral Rock in the distance. Continue north as the trail descends to Oak Creek, crosses the ditch, and then turns southeast to follow the creek. At the junction with the Kisva Trail, you've completed the loop. Retrace your steps to return to the visitor center.

2
MORMON CANYON

Description: A hike to the towering sandstone cliffs and spires on the west side of Wilson Mountain, in the Red Rock–Secret Mountain Wilderness.
Location: Northeast Sedona.
Type of trail: Out-and-back.
Difficulty: Moderate.
Total distance: 4.2 miles.
High point: 4,900 feet.
Elevation change: 640 feet.
Time required: 3 hours.
Water: None.
Best season: All year.
Maps: Wilson Mountain USGS quad; Coconino National Forest.
Permits and restrictions: A Red Rock Pass is required for vehicle parking.
For more information: Sedona Ranger District, Coconino National Forest; (928) 282–4119.

Finding the trailhead: From the junction of Arizona 89A and AZ 179 in Sedona, drive north on AZ 89A about 0.4 mile, and then turn left onto Jordan Road. After 0.8 mile turn left on Park Ridge Road and continue to the trailhead at a locked gate (the last 0.2 mile is dirt).

Mormon Canyon

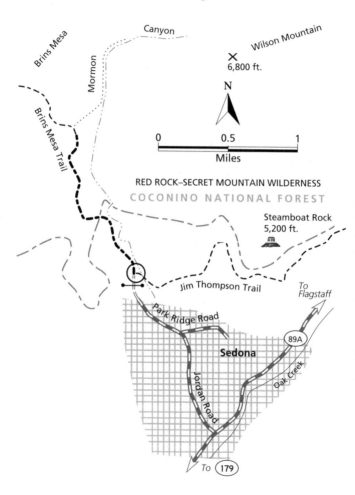

Key points:
0.0 Trailhead.
1.4 Follow cairns northeast.
2.1 Head of Mormon Canyon.

The hike: Go past the gate and continue past the old shooting range on the Brins Mesa Trail. This trail works its way through the Arizona cypress forest along the west side of Mormon Canyon. Arizona cypress is easily identified by its curly red bark and juniperlike scaly needles. It is a survivor of past climate change and now grows only in isolated pockets below the western Mogollon Rim and in the central mountains of Arizona. As the trail starts to climb toward Brins Mesa, visible on the skyline to the north, watch for a cairned route that turns off to the right (northeast). Leave the trail and follow the cairns across the red sandstone ledges of the Schnebly Hill formation. The route descends into the bed of Mormon Canyon and follows it upstream. Without much difficulty you can get very close to the beautiful cliffs of Wilson Mountain. The head of Mormon Canyon offers a surprisingly remote feeling, considering its proximity to Sedona.

3
JIM THOMPSON TRAIL

Description: A short hike south of Wilson Mountain with spectacular views of Steamboat Rock, lower Oak Creek Canyon, and Mitten Ridge.
Location: Northeast Sedona.
Type of trail: Out-and-back.
Difficulty: Easy.
Total distance: 4.0 miles.
High point: 4,800 feet.
Elevation change: 200 feet.
Time required: 2.5 hours.
Water: None.
Best season: All year.
Maps: Wilson Mountain, Munds Park USGS quads; Coconino National Forest.
Permits and restrictions: A Red Rock Pass is required for vehicle parking on the national forest.
For more information: Sedona Ranger District, Coconino National Forest; (928) 282–4119.

Finding the trailhead: From the junction of Arizona 89A and AZ 179 in Sedona, drive north on AZ 89A about 0.4 mile, and then turn left onto Jordan Road. After 0.8 mile turn left on Park Ridge Road, and continue to the trailhead at a locked gate (the last 0.2 mile is dirt).

Jim Thompson Trail

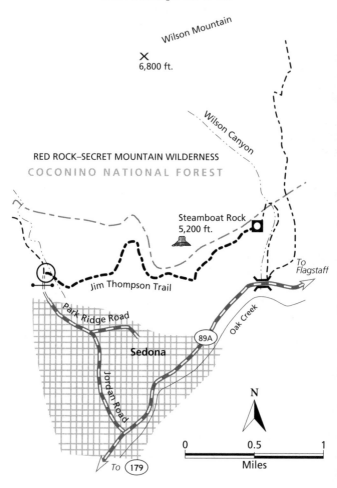

Wilson Mountain

✕
6,800 ft.

Wilson Canyon

RED ROCK–SECRET MOUNTAIN WILDERNESS
COCONINO NATIONAL FOREST

Steamboat Rock
5,200 ft.

Jim Thompson Trail

To
Flagstaff

Park Ridge Road

89A

Oak Creek

Sedona

Jordan Road

To 179

N

0   0.5   1
Miles

Key points:
0.0 Trailhead.
0.7 Base of Steamboat Rock.
2.0 Wilson Canyon overlook.

The hike: Go through the gate, and then turn right on the Jim Thompson Trail, which crosses the bed of Mormon Canyon and then swings northeast. You'll be heading directly for Steamboat Rock, the southernmost ridge of Wilson Mountain. When the trail reaches the base of the red sandstone cliffs, it turns east and contours along ledges. After passing the eastern end of Steamboat Rock, the trail reaches a viewpoint overlooking Wilson Canyon and lower Oak Creek. This is a great ending for an easy hike, though the trail does continue to the bottom of Wilson Canyon. See *Hiking Northern Arizona* for information on connecting trails.

4
HUCKABY TRAIL

Description: A fine day hike on a trail on the Coconino National Forest that follows Oak Creek for part of the way.
Location: 2.0 miles east of Sedona.
Type of trail: Out-and-back (can be done one way with a car shuttle).
Difficulty: Moderate.
Total distance: 5.0 miles.
High point: 4,520 feet.
Elevation change: 260 feet.
Time required: 3 hours.
Water: Oak Creek.
Best season: All year.
Maps: Munds Park, Munds Mountain, Sedona USGS quads; Coconino National Forest.
Permits and restrictions: A Red Rock Pass is required for vehicle parking.
For more information: Sedona Ranger District, Coconino National Forest; (928) 282–4119.

Finding the trailhead: From the junction of Arizona 89A and AZ 179 in Sedona, go south 0.4 mile on AZ 179, across Oak Creek Bridge, and then turn left on Schnebly Hill Road (Forest Road 152). Drive 1.9 miles, and then turn

Huckaby Trail

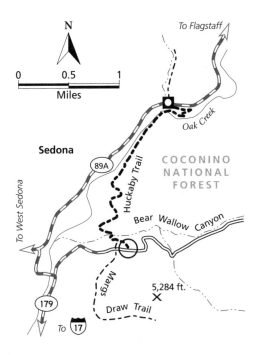

left into Margs Draw/Huckaby Trailhead. To reach the north trailhead from the junction of AZ 89A and AZ 179 in Sedona, drive 1.6 miles north on AZ 89A, cross Midgely Bridge, and park on the left at the Wilson Canyon Trailhead and viewpoint.

Key points:
0.0 Margs Draw/ Huckaby Trailhead.
0.3 Bear Wallow Canyon.
1.5 Oak Creek.
2.1 Cross Oak Creek.
2.5 Viewpoint at the Wilson Canyon Trailhead.

The hike: The first section of the Huckaby Trail goes west, loosely paralleling the Schnebly Hill Road. After the Margs Draw Trail junction, the trail turns right and follows an old road down into Bear Wallow Canyon (the canyon north of the trailhead). Follow the old road across this normally dry canyon and out the north side. Here a newer foot trail leaves the old road and contours northeast above the canyon. Soon a switchback takes you to the north as the trail begins to work its way toward Oak Creek. This is a delightful traverse through pinyon-juniper forest, though it would be hot on a summer afternoon. Soon you'll start to descend, and the trail finally switchbacks down to Oak Creek. The trail stays on the east side of the creek for 0.5 mile, giving you access to the creek at several points. Below Midgely Bridge, the impressive structure spanning Mormon Canyon on AZ 89A, the trail crosses to the west side of the creek. Now it follows an old wagon road that climbs steeply out of the canyon and switchbacks up to the north end of the bridge. Your hike ends at the viewpoint next to the bridge—a spot that offers excellent views of the portion of Oak Creek that you just hiked.

5
MUNDS MOUNTAIN TRAIL

Description: This hike in the Munds Mountain Wilderness takes you up a historic, closed road and offers excellent views of Mitten Ridge, Bear Wallow Canyon, Munds Mountain, and Sedona.
Location: 4.0 miles east of Sedona.
Type of trail: Out-and-back.
Difficulty: Moderate.
Total distance: 4.2 miles.
High point: 6,830 feet.
Elevation change: 1,200 feet.
Time required: 3 hours.
Water: None.
Best season: April through November.
Maps: Munds Park, Munds Mountain USGS quads; Coconino National Forest.
Permits and restrictions: A Red Rock Pass is required for vehicle parking.
For more information: Sedona Ranger District, Coconino National Forest; (928) 282–4119.

Finding the trailhead: From the junction of Arizona 89A and AZ 179 in Sedona, go south 0.4 mile on AZ 179, across Oak Creek Bridge, and then turn left on Schnebly Hill Road (Forest Road 152). Drive 4.3 miles, and park at the

Munds Mountain Trail

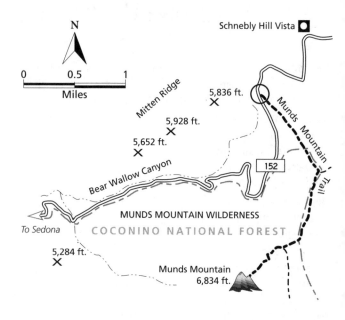

unsigned trailhead where the road passes through a saddle between the red buttes to the west and the brushy slope on the right.

Key points:
0.0 Trailhead.
0.9 Continue south on the foot trail.

1.8 Saddle.
2.1 Munds Mountain.

The hike: From the parking area look across the road and up. You will see an old road descending the slopes from the left (southeast). It nearly comes down to the present road and then does a switchback to the right and parallels the road. Walk south down the main road about 100 yards until you can climb up to reach the old road. Follow the old road back to the left (north), around the switchback, and then southward. This is the old Schnebly Hill Road, a former wagon road that connected Sedona to Flagstaff via the Mogollon Rim. It is now closed to motorized vehicles and makes a fine hiking trail with a panoramic view. Because of the west-facing slope, the dominant vegetation is chaparral brush. Near the top there is a dense stand of Gambel oaks, small, slender deciduous trees about 20 feet tall. Gambel oaks favor the slopes just below escarpments or rims. The trail reaches the Mogollon Rim after 0.9 mile, and the old road turns sharply north.

Take the foot trail, which continues south along the rim through tall ponderosa pines, climbing gradually. About 0.7 mile from the old road, the trail reaches a high point and crosses a grassy section with scattered juniper trees where the view opens out to the southeast. The long ridge of Munds Mountain dominates the view ahead to the southwest. The trail drops down a short ridge to a saddle where there is a junction with the Hot Loop Trail to the left. Continue straight ahead about 50 yards to another saddle where there is a junction with the Jacks Canyon Trail.

Stay right and follow the Munds Mountain Trail as it climbs steeply up the northeast slopes. Several switchbacks lead to a ridge where the grade moderates. This section is interesting because of the extreme contrast in vegetation on the two sides of the ridge. Douglas-fir growing on the north slopes meet pinyons, junipers, and Arizona cypresses growing on the south slopes. The trail reaches the rim of Munds Mountain about 0.4 mile from the junction at the saddle. According to the topo map the actual high point is about 100 yards south along the east edge of the clearing. But it is more rewarding to walk about 200 yards west to the rim for a sweeping view of Sedona and the Red Rock Country. You can also walk about 100 yards to the north rim for a superb view of lower Oak Creek Canyon and nearly the entire trail you just came up.

6
LITTLE HORSE TRAIL

Description: An easily reached hike that goes past the dramatic Chapel Rocks to a scenic overlook.
Location: Southeast Sedona.
Type of trail: Out-and-back.
Difficulty: Easy.
Total distance: 3.6 miles.
High point: 4,600 feet.
Elevation change: 280 feet.
Time required: 2 hours.
Water: None.
Best season: All year.
Maps: Sedona USGS quad.
Permits and restrictions: A Red Rock Pass is required for vehicle parking.
For more information: Sedona Ranger District, Coconino National Forest; (928) 282–4119.

Finding the trailhead: From the junction of Arizona 89A and AZ 179 in Sedona, go 3.5 miles south on AZ 179 and park at the North Bell Rock Pathway Trailhead, on the left.

Key points:
0.0 North Bell Rock Pathway Trailhead.
0.3 Turn left onto the Little Horse Trail.
1.8 Chicken Point.

Little Horse Trail

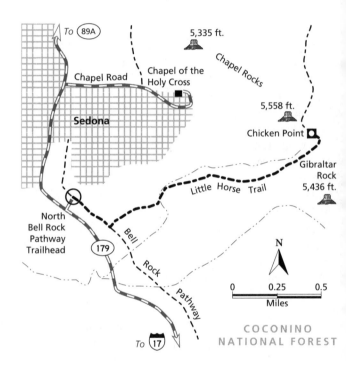

The hike: This short but scenic hike uses part of the urban trail system in Sedona. From the trailhead turn right on the Bell Rock Pathway. After 0.3 mile turn left on the Little Horse Trail. This trail is marked with rock cairns in wire cages. Ignore the numerous unmarked side trails and follow the cairns to Chicken Point, which is actually the pass between the Chapel Rocks and Gibraltar Rock. Surrounded by the towering red rocks of the Schnebly Hill formation, this scenic spot is a fine place to relax and enjoy the view.

7
COURTHOUSE BUTTE LOOP

Description: A day hike in and near the Munds Mountain Wilderness, offering close-up views of two of Sedona's famous landmark rock formations, Bell Rock and Courthouse Butte.
Location: 5.0 miles south of Sedona.
Type of trail: Loop.
Difficulty: Easy.
Total distance: 4.3 miles.
High point: 4,460 feet.
Elevation change: 200 feet.
Time required: 2.5 hours.
Water: None.
Best season: All year.
Maps: Sedona, Munds Mountain USGS quads; Coconino National Forest.
Permits and restrictions: A Red Rock Pass is required for vehicle parking.
For more information: Sedona Ranger District, Coconino National Forest; (928) 282–4119.

Finding the trailhead: From the junction of Arizona 89A and AZ 179 in Sedona, go 6.0 miles south on AZ 179, and then turn left into the South Bell Rock Pathway Trailhead.

Courthouse Butte Loop

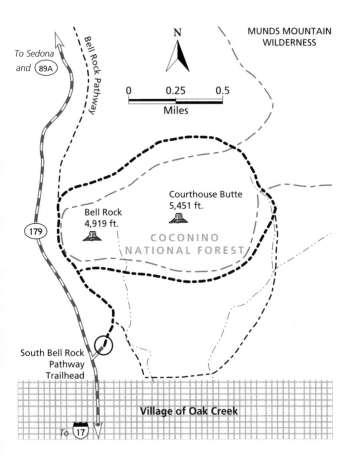

Key points:
0.0 South Bell Rock Pathway Trailhead.
1.0 Turn right on an old jeep road.
2.1 Pass northeast of Courthouse Butte.
2.7 Cross a wash, and then turn right.
3.8 Turn left on the Bell Rock Pathway.
4.3 South Bell Rock Pathway Trailhead.

The hike: Don't let the crowds of windshield tourists at the trailhead put you off. You'll soon leave them and the roar of the highway behind. Follow the broad Bell Rock Pathway north toward Bell Rock. The trail squeezes between Bell Rock and the highway. Turn right on an old, closed jeep trail that heads around the north side of Bell Rock. After about 0.5 mile the jeep trail veers left (northeast), descends into a drainage, and crosses it. At this point turn right (east) and stay in the drainage, following a foot trail that climbs gradually toward the pass east of Courthouse Rock, the massive butte east of Bell Rock. From the pass follow the trail as it descends the drainage to the southeast. About 0.5 mile from the pass, the trail meets an unsigned trail that crosses the dry streambed. Turn right (west) on this trail and continue around Courthouse Butte. The trail comes out onto a flat where the view is more open and stays just at the base of Courthouse Butte. Numerous trails branch left; go right at each junction. Back near the highway, you'll pass the cottonwood trees that mark Bell Rock Spring, which is not a reliable water source, and then meet the Bell Rock Pathway. Turn left to return to the trailhead.

OAK CREEK CANYON

8
COOKSTOVE TRAIL

Description: This short trail offers unique views of upper Oak Creek Canyon.
Location: 13.0 miles north of Sedona.
Type of trail: Out-and-back.
Difficulty: Moderate.
Total distance: 1.0 mile.
High point: 6,320 feet.
Elevation change: 940 feet.
Time required: 1 hour.
Water: None.
Best season: April through November.
Maps: Mountainaire USGS quad; Coconino National Forest.
Permits and restrictions: A Red Rock Pass is required for vehicle parking.
For more information: Sedona Ranger District, Coconino National Forest; (928) 282–4119.

Cookstove Trail, Harding Spring Trail, Thomas Point Trail, West Fork Trail, AB Young Trail

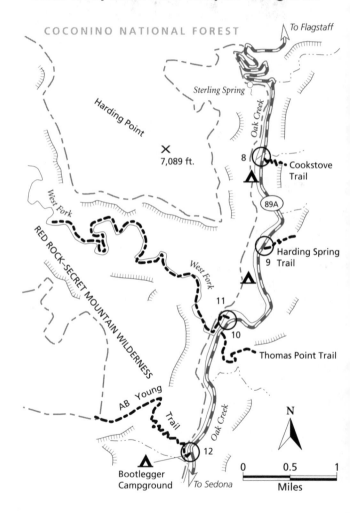

Finding the trailhead: From Sedona drive about 13.0 miles north on Arizona 89A to the north end of Pine Flat Campground, and park along the highway.

Key points:
0.0 Pine Flat Campground.
0.5 East rim of Oak Creek Canyon.

The hike: Like most of the old trails in Oak Creek Canyon, this trail is not shown on the topographic map. The trail starts just north of the Pine Flat Campground on the east side of the highway. It climbs directly up the ridge just south of Cookstove Draw. Although the trail is steep, it has been maintained in recent years and is in good shape. There are good views of upper Oak Creek Canyon, which is heavily forested with ponderosa pine, Gambel oak, and Douglas-fir. Alligator junipers are also common and are easily identified by their bark, which is broken into deep squares like an alligator's hide. Some alligator junipers reach massive sizes. The trail, originally built for fire-fighting access, reaches the east rim of Oak Creek Canyon just south of Cookstove Draw.

9
HARDING SPRING TRAIL

see map page 34

Description: A cool, shady hike through ponderosa-pine and Douglas-fir forest to the east rim of Oak Creek canyon.
Location: 12.0 miles north of Sedona.
Type of trail: Out-and-back.
Difficulty: Moderate.
Total distance: 1.4 miles.
High point: 6,200 feet.
Elevation change: 750 feet.
Time required: 1.5 hours.
Water: None.
Best season: April through November.
Maps: Mountainaire USGS quad; Coconino National Forest.
Permits and restrictions: A Red Rock Pass is required for vehicle parking.
For more information: Sedona Ranger District, Coconino National Forest; (928) 282–4119.

Finding the trailhead: From Sedona drive about 12.0 miles north on Arizona 89A to the Cave Springs Campground turnoff. (The campground sign may not be present during winter, when the campground is closed.) The turnoff is on the left (west); park in the pullout just to the north.

Key points:
0.0 Trailhead.
0.7 East rim of Oak Creek Canyon.

The hike: Walk across the highway to reach the sign that marks the start of the trail. The trail immediately turns left and starts to climb. (Ignore the trail that heads to the right and parallels the highway.) Originally built by the early settlers as a route to move their cattle to the forested plateau above, the Harding Spring Trail is still in good shape, and you'll see sections of elaborate trail construction. The trail climbs north across the slope, leaving the busy highway far below, and then a final series of switchbacks lead to the east rim of Oak Creek Canyon. The trail continues south along the rim for 100 yards to a viewpoint overlooking the canyon. Here you can clearly see that the west rim is quite a bit higher than the rim you're standing on. This is due to the Oak Creek Fault, which resulted when the west rim was raised. In the process the fault fractured and weakened the rock, allowing water erosion to carve out Oak Creek Canyon.

10
THOMAS POINT TRAIL

see map page 34

Description: This hike is a great alternative to the crowded West Fork Trail (Hike 11), and it's located right across the highway. There are excellent views of the West Fork of Oak Creek, and of Oak Creek Canyon itself.

Location: 11.0 miles north of Sedona.

Type of trail: Out-and-back.

Difficulty: Moderate.

Total distance: 2.0 miles.

High point: 6,275 feet.

Elevation change: 970 feet.

Time required: 2 hours.

Water: None.

Best season: April through November.

Maps: Munds Park USGS quad; Coconino National Forest.

Permits and restrictions: A Red Rock Pass is required for vehicle parking, in addition to the parking fee at the West Fork Trailhead.

For more information: Sedona Ranger District, Coconino National Forest; (928) 282–4119.

Finding the trailhead: From Sedona drive about 11.0 miles north on Arizona 89A, and then turn left into the West Fork Trailhead.

Key points:
0.0 Trailhead.
0.4 The trail emerges onto the south-facing slope.
1.0 East rim of Oak Creek Canyon.

The hike: From the parking area follow the trail south through the old orchard for about 100 yards and cross the highway to the Thomas Point trail sign. The trail climbs south through a shady forest of ponderosa pine and Gambel oak, and then turns a corner onto a much drier, south-facing slope. Here, because of the increased temperature and evaporation, the chaparral plants dominate: scrub oak, mountain mahogany, and manzanita. There are fine views down the canyon to the flat-topped mesa of Wilson Mountain. A switchback leads to a point overlooking the mouth of the West Fork, and then the trail turns east again and climbs into a pine-covered saddle. The trail finishes by following the ridge east 100 yards to the rim, where views are limited because of the thick forest. You'll find a better viewpoint by walking about 100 yards west from the saddle, onto a rock outcrop. Here you're looking directly up the West Fork of Oak Creek.

11
WEST FORK TRAIL

see map page 34

Description: An easy, very popular hike through the spectacular West Fork of Oak Creek, in the Red Rock–Secret Mountain Wilderness.

Location: 11.0 miles north of Sedona.

Type of trail: Out-and-back.

Difficulty: Easy.

Total distance: 6.0 miles.

High point: 5,600 feet.

Elevation change: 300 feet.

Time required: 3 hours.

Water: West Fork.

Best season: April through November.

Maps: Dutton Hill, Wilson Mountain, Munds Park USGS quads; Coconino National Forest.

Permits and restrictions: A Red Rock Pass is required for vehicle parking, in addition to the parking fee at the West Fork Trailhead. The lower 6.0 miles of the West Fork is closed to camping due to heavy use.

For more information: Sedona Ranger District, Coconino National Forest; (928) 282–4119.

Finding the trailhead: From Sedona drive about 11.0 miles north on Arizona 89A, and then turn left into the West Fork Trailhead parking area.

Key points:
0.0 Trailhead.
0.4 Mouth of the West Fork.
3.0 Trail ends.

The hike: The West Fork is an easy but extremely popular hike. It is not the place to go to escape crowds, especially on weekends. For solitude try the Thomas Point Trail (Hike 10) on the opposite side of Oak Creek. Note that the Forest Service prohibits camping in the lower West Fork due to heavy use. Stay on the trail and do not pick flowers or otherwise disturb this fragile environment. Watch for poison ivy, a low plant that is common along the trail. The sap of this plant contains an acid that causes a skin reaction in most people. If you suspect you've been in contact, wash the affected area immediately with water. Poison ivy is easily recognized by its shiny leaves, which grow in clusters of three.

Follow the trail across Oak Creek. From here the trail goes south along the creek and then turns right (west) into the West Fork. Soon you'll leave the sounds of the busy highway behind and be able to hear the pleasant murmur of the creek and the whisper of the wind in the trees. Buttresses of Coconino sandstone tower on the left, while the canyon floor is filled with an exceptionally tall ponderosa-pine and Douglas-fir forest. The trail crosses the creek several times and ends about 3.0 miles up the canyon. This is the turnaround point for the easy hike. Beyond the end of the trail, the canyon is often flooded wall-to-wall, requiring canyoneering skills to negotiate.

12
AB YOUNG TRAIL

see map page 34

Description: This is a good trail to the west rim of Oak Creek Canyon, in the Red Rock–Secret Mountain Wilderness. It offers the best views of Oak Creek Canyon from any of the rim trails.

Location: 9.0 miles north of Sedona.

Type of trail: Out-and-back.

Difficulty: Moderate.

Total distance: 4.4 miles.

High point: 7,196 feet.

Elevation change: 2,000 feet.

Time required: 5 hours.

Water: None.

Best season: April through November.

Maps: Munds Park, Wilson Mountain USGS quads; Coconino National Forest.

Permits and restrictions: A Red Rock Pass is required for vehicle parking.

For more information: Sedona Ranger District, Coconino National Forest; (928) 282–4119.

Finding the trailhead: From Sedona drive about 9.0 miles north on Arizona 89A to the Bootlegger Campground. Do not block the campground entrance; park in the highway pullout just to the north.

Key points:
0.0 Trailhead at Bootlegger Campground.
1.4 West Rim of Oak Creek Canyon.
1.8 Trail leaves rim.
2.2 East Pocket Lookout.

The hike: Walk through the campground and cross Oak Creek. Turn left (south) on the trail that parallels the creek, and watch for the AB Young Trail, a good, maintained trail that turns sharply right and starts climbing to the northwest. The broad-leafed trees in the riparian habitat along the creek are soon left behind as the trail climbs through ponderosa-pine forest. After a short distance the trail begins switchbacking directly up the steep slope. The dry southwest exposure supports dense chaparral brush, and the view opens up as you climb. Just below the rim the trail veers north in a long final switchback. At the rim the trail enters pine forest again. Turn southwest and follow the cairned trail, which is fainter, along the pine-forested rim to the crest of an east–west ridge. Here the trail turns west and follows the flat-topped ridge to East Pocket Knob and the end of the trail at the Forest Service fire tower. Get permission from the lookout before climbing the tower for a panoramic view of the Mogollon Rim and Oak Creek Canyon.

The AB Young Trail was originally built to move cattle to and from the rim country; it was improved by the Civilian Conservation Corps in the 1930s. The CCC, along with several other conservation agencies, built thousands of miles of trails in the national forests and parks during this period.

13
STERLING PASS

Description: A less-used trail below the impressive cliffs of the north face of Wilson Mountain, in the Red Rock–Secret Mountain Wilderness.
Location: 6.0 miles north of Sedona.
Type of trail: Out-and-back.
Difficulty: Moderate.
Total distance: 1.8 miles.
High point: 5,980 feet.
Elevation change: 1,160 feet.
Time required: 2 hours.
Water: None.
Best season: April through November.
Maps: Munds Park, Wilson Mountain USGS quads; Coconino National Forest.
Permits and restrictions: A Red Rock Pass is required for vehicle parking.
For more information: Sedona Ranger District, Coconino National Forest; (928) 282–4119.

Finding the trailhead: From Sedona drive about 6.0 miles north on Arizona 89A to the Manzanita Campground. The trail starts from the west side of the highway just north of the campground, but parking is very limited. You

Sterling Pass

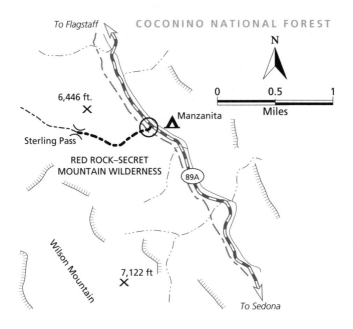

may have to park at the pullouts south of the campground and walk through the campground to reach the trailhead.

Key points:
0.0 Trailhead.
0.9 Sterling Pass.

The hike: After leaving the highway, the Sterling Pass Trail climbs steeply up a drainage and through a fine stand of ponderosa pines. It skirts a dry waterfall and begins a series of short, steep switchbacks. There are occasional views of the massive cliffs that form the north side of Wilson Mountain. The hike ends at Sterling Pass, the sharp notch between the Mogollon Rim and Wilson Mountain.

14
NORTH WILSON
MOUNTAIN TRAIL

Description: This is a good hike on a hot day since much of the trail is in a north-facing, shady canyon in the Red Rock–Secret Mountain Wilderness. You'll have excellent views of Oak Creek Canyon from the First Bench of Wilson Mountain.

Location: 5.0 miles north of Sedona.

Type of trail: Out-and-back.

Difficulty: Moderate.

Total distance: 2.8 miles.

High point: 6,160 feet.

Elevation change: 1,400 feet.

Time required: 3 hours.

Water: None.

Best season: April through November.

Maps: Munds Park, Wilson Mountain USGS quads; Coconino National Forest.

Permits and restrictions: A Red Rock Pass is required for vehicle parking.

For more information: Sedona Ranger District, Coconino National Forest; (928) 282–4119.

Finding the trailhead: From Sedona drive about 5.0 miles north on Arizona 89A to the Encinoso Picnic Area. Park in the trailhead parking area at the entrance to the picnic area.

North Wilson Mountain Trail

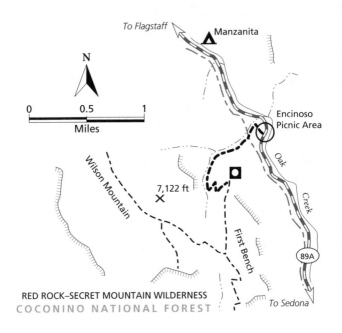

Key points:

0.0 North Wilson Mountain Trailhead.
1.4 First Bench of Wilson Mountain.

The hike: The trailhead is signed, although the North Wilson Mountain Trail is not shown on the topographic map.

The trail starts climbing immediately through mixed chaparral, ponderosa-pine, and oak forest. When the trail reaches the ridge above the picnic area, it turns to the south and follows the ridge a short distance, giving you good views of Oak Creek Canyon. After leaving the ridge the trail climbs southwest up a heavily wooded drainage. The shade of the large ponderosa pines is a welcome relief on hot days. As the trail nears the base of the massive, buff-colored Coconino sandstone cliffs, it crosses the drainage and begins to switchback up the slope to the east. There are more fine views when the trail reaches the ridge at the top of this slope. The trail turns to the south again and follows the ridge onto the First Bench of Wilson Mountain, the goal for your hike. You're on a gently sloping volcanic plateau level with the east rim of Oak Creek Canyon. Walk out to a rocky viewpoint a few yards to the east for great views up Oak Creek Canyon. (The trail continues to the top of Wilson Mountain, which is a much longer hike. See *Hiking Northern Arizona* for details.)

15
ALLENS BEND TRAIL

Description: Although short, the Allens Bend Trail is a pleasant walk and one of the few trails along Oak Creek. This trail is especially fine in the fall, when the riparian forest is vibrant with fall color.

Location: 2.0 miles north of Sedona.

Type of trail: Out-and-back.

Difficulty: Easy.

Total distance: 0.6 mile.

High point: 4,440 feet.

Elevation change: None.

Time required: 0.5 hour.

Water: Oak Creek.

Best season: All year.

Maps: Munds Park USGS quad; Coconino National Forest.

Permits and restrictions: A Red Rock Pass is required for vehicle parking. There is an additional fee for use of the Grasshopper Point parking area.

For more information: Sedona Ranger District, Coconino National Forest; (928) 282–4119.

Finding the trailhead: From Sedona drive about 2.0 miles north on Arizona 89A, and then turn right (east) into the Grasshopper Point Picnic Area.

Allens Bend Trail, Wilson Mountain Trail, Wilson Canyon

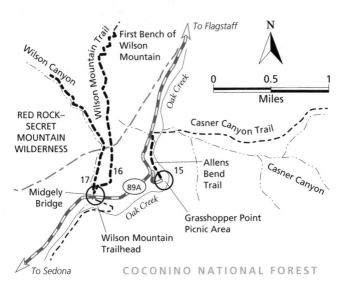

Key points:
0.0 Trailhead.
0.3 End of trail.

The hike: The trail starts from the north end of the parking lot and follows the west bank of Oak Creek. There are several sections of elaborate trail construction near the beginning, and then the trail comes out onto a wider bench.

Watch for poison ivy, which is very common along Oak Creek. The trail ends near an old road that comes down from the highway above. Even though it is short, the Allens Bend Trail is a pleasant, shady walk along the rushing waters of Oak Creek.

In this area the red rocks near the creek are shales, sandstones, and limestones of the Supai formation. The Supai begins to outcrop here and forms the inner gorge of Oak Creek Canyon below this point. These mixed rock formations resulted from a fluctuating near-shore marine environment, in which deep-sea limestones were laid down alternately with shallow-water shale and sandstones.

16
WILSON MOUNTAIN TRAIL

see map page 51

Description: This popular hike climbs the south slopes of Wilson Mountain in the Red Rock–Secret Mountain Wilderness. Your reward for the effort is an excellent view of lower Oak Creek Canyon.

Location: 2.0 miles north of Sedona.

Type of trail: Out-and-back.

Difficulty: Moderate.

Total distance: 4.4 miles.

High point: 6,180 feet.

Elevation change: 1,680 feet.

Time required: 4 hours.

Water: None. The trail faces south and is hot in summer; bring plenty of water.

Best season: All year.

Maps: Wilson Mountain, Munds Park USGS quads; Coconino National Forest.

Permits and restrictions: A Red Rock Pass is required for vehicle parking.

For more information: Sedona Ranger District, Coconino National Forest; (928) 282–4119.

Finding the trailhead: From Sedona drive 1.6 miles north on Arizona 89A, cross Midgely Bridge, and then turn left into the Wilson Mountain Trailhead and viewpoint.

Key points:

0.0 Wilson Mountain Trailhead.

2.2 First Bench of Wilson Mountain.

The hike: The Wilson Mountain Trail starts climbing immediately, but then the climb moderates for a bit as the trail goes north through open pinyon-juniper forest. The climb starts in earnest as the trail starts switchbacking up the steep, south-facing slopes. The view opens up as the pigmy forest is replaced by the chaparral brush that favors this sun-baked slope. The trail reaches the First Bench of Wilson Mountain, your goal for this hike. You can walk southeast along the rim of this sloping volcanic shelf to a viewpoint overlooking lower Oak Creek Canyon and the magnificent red-rock formations surrounding uptown Sedona. (The trail continues to the top of Wilson Mountain, which is a more difficult hike. See *Hiking Northern Arizona* for details.)

17
WILSON CANYON

see map page 51

Description: An easy, popular walk up a red-rock canyon in the Red Rock–Secret Mountain Wilderness.
Location: 2.0 miles north of Sedona.
Type of trail: Out-and-back.
Difficulty: Easy.
Total distance: 2.0 miles.
High point: 4,940 feet.
Elevation change: 440 feet.
Time required: 1.5 hours.
Water: None.
Best season: All year.
Maps: Munds Park USGS quad; Coconino National Forest.
Permits and restrictions: A Red Rock Pass is required for vehicle parking.
For more information: Sedona Ranger District, Coconino National Forest; (928) 282–4119.

Finding the trailhead: From Sedona drive 1.6 miles north on Arizona 89A, cross Midgely Bridge, and then turn left into the Wilson Mountain Trailhead and viewpoint.

Key points:
0.0 Wilson Mountain Trailhead.
1.0 End of trail.

The hike: The Wilson Canyon Trail starts from the north end of the parking area and stays near the rim of the inner canyon. After this gorge ends at a high, dry waterfall, the Jim Thompson Trail branches left. The trail wanders another 0.5 mile up the canyon though fine stands of Arizona cypress before fading out.

RED ROCK CANYONS

18
DOGIE TRAIL

Description: This is a fine hike through the remote red-rock canyons of the Sycamore Canyon and Red Rock–Secret Mountain Wildernesses.

Location: 19.0 miles west of Sedona.

Type of trail: Out-and-back.

Difficulty: Moderate.

Total distance: 9.8 miles.

High point: 4,920 feet.

Elevation change: 700 feet.

Time required: 6–7 hours.

Water: Seasonal in Sycamore Creek.

Best season: March through November.

Maps: Sycamore Point, Sycamore Basin, Loy Butte USGS quads; Coconino National Forest.

Permits and restrictions: A Red Rock Pass is required for vehicle parking.

For more information: Sedona Ranger District, Coconino National Forest; (928) 282–4119.

Dogie Trail, Robbers Roost

Finding the trailhead: From Sedona drive about 8.0 miles south on Arizona 89A, and then turn right (northwest) on Forest Road 525, a maintained dirt road. Go 2.2 miles, and then turn left (west) onto FR 525C. Continue 8.8 miles to the end of the road at the Dogie Trailhead. The last mile or two frequently washes out and may be very rough, but the rest is passable to ordinary cars.

Key points:
0.0 Dogie Trailhead.
0.4 Sycamore Pass.
4.9 Sycamore Creek.

The hike: The start of the Dogie Trail is shown on the Loy Butte quad, but the trail is missing from the adjoining Sycamore Basin quad. You'll climb a short distance to cross Sycamore Pass and then descend gradually to the west. The trail turns north and works its way along a sloping terrace through pinyon-juniper forest. The inner gorge of Sycamore Canyon is visible to the west, and the cliffs of Casner Mountain rise on the east. Eventually, the trail descends to Sycamore Creek, which is the goal for your hike. Sycamore Canyon is a large, remote canyon system, which offers plenty of opportunities for extended exploration (see *Hiking Northern Arizona* for more information). This portion of Sycamore Creek is usually dry during summer and fall but may be flooding during the early spring snowmelt.

19
ROBBERS ROOST

see map page 58

Description: This is a very easy walk to a scenic red-rock overlook and a small cave in the Coconino National Forest. According to local lore the cave was once an outlaw hideout.

Location: 19.0 miles west of Sedona.

Type of trail: Out-and-back.

Difficulty: Easy.

Total distance: 0.6 mile.

High point: 5,110 feet.

Elevation change: None.

Time required: 30 minutes.

Water: None.

Best season: All year.

Maps: Loy Butte USGS quad; Coconino National Forest.

Permits and restrictions: A Red Rock Pass is required for vehicle parking.

For more information: Sedona Ranger District, Coconino National Forest; (928) 282–4119.

Finding the trailhead: From Sedona drive west about 8.0 miles on Arizona 89A, and then turn right (northwest) on Forest Road 525, a maintained dirt road. Go 2.2 miles, and then turn left (west) at a sign for FR 525C. Continue 7.5 miles, and then turn right (north) on an unmaintained road that climbs up a ridge toward the east side of Casner

Mountain. (Casner Mountain can be identified by the power line that runs down its south slopes.) Go 1.1 miles up this road until you are directly west of Robbers Roost, a low red-rock mesa across the gully to the right (east). The trailhead and trail are unmarked.

Key points:
0.0 Trailhead.
0.3 Robbers Roost.

The hike: Follow an unmarked trail (not shown on the topographic map) across the shallow gully and up to the north side of Robbers Roost. Then traverse a red sandstone ledge around to a cave on the east side of the rock, just below the rim. Inside the cave a small wall was supposedly built by robbers for defense. The main attraction, however, is the picture-window view of Secret Mountain, Bear Mountain, and the Sedona area from within the cave. A hole though a small fin provides a smaller window. It is also interesting to explore the top of this small mesa. After a rain there will be temporary water pockets that reflect the sky and the red rocks.

20
LOY CANYON

Description: A scenic hike up a red-rock canyon to the Mogollon Rim in the Red Rock–Secret Mountain Wilderness.

Location: 12.0 miles northwest of Sedona.

Type of trail: Out-and-back.

Difficulty: Moderate.

Total distance: 9.6 miles out and back.

High point: 6,620 feet.

Elevation change: 1,900 feet.

Time required: 6 hours.

Water: None.

Best season: All year.

Maps: Loy Butte USGS quad; Coconino National Forest.

Permits and restrictions: A Red Rock Pass is required for vehicle parking.

For more information: Sedona Ranger District, Coconino National Forest; (928) 282–4119.

Finding the trailhead: From Sedona drive to the west end of town on Arizona 89A, and then turn right at a traffic light onto Dry Creek Road. Drive 2.8 miles, and then turn left onto Boynton Canyon Road. Continue 1.6 miles, and then turn left onto Forest Road 152C, a maintained dirt road. After 3.0 miles turn right onto FR 525. Continue 3.7 miles to the Loy Canyon Trailhead. (If you have gone too far, you will see the Hancock Ranch to the right.)

Loy Canyon

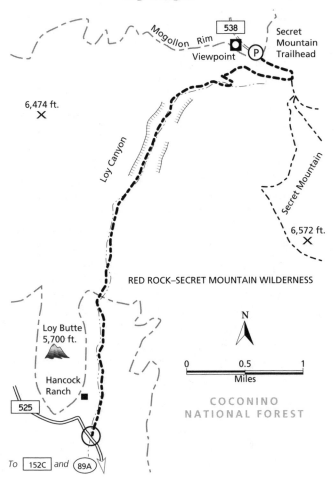

Mogollon Rim

538

Secret Mountain Trailhead

Viewpoint

P

6,474 ft.
×

Loy Canyon

Secret Mountain

6,572 ft.
×

RED ROCK–SECRET MOUNTAIN WILDERNESS

Loy Butte
5,700 ft.

Hancock Ranch

525

To 152C and 89A

N

0   0.5   1
Miles

COCONINO
NATIONAL FOREST

Key points:
0.0 Loy Canyon Trailhead.
2.1 Red-rock narrows.
3.0 End of narrows.
4.4 Junction with Secret Mountain Trail; turn left.
4.8 Secret Mountain Trailhead.

The hike: Initially the trail skirts the Hancock Ranch along the ranch's east boundary. After passing the ranch the trail then joins the dry creek bed, which it follows northward through the open pinyon-pine, juniper, and Arizona-cypress forest. Conical Loy Butte looms to the west, and the cliffs of Secret Mountain tower over Loy Canyon on the east. After 2.1 miles the canyon becomes narrower, and the trail turns slightly toward the northeast. In another mile the trail turns toward the east as the canyon opens up a bit. The buff-colored Coconino sandstone cliffs of the Mogollon Rim tower above the trail to the north, and matching cliffs form the north end of Secret Mountain. This scenic spot makes a good stopping point for those hikers who desire an easy hike.

If you continue, watch carefully for the point where the trail leaves the canyon bottom and begins climbing the north side of the canyon in a series of switchbacks. Though it is a steep climb, the reward is an expanding view of Loy Canyon. Notice the contrast between the brushy vegetation on this dry, south-facing slope and the cool, moist pine and fir forest across the canyon to the south.

The Loy Canyon Trail ends where it joins the Secret Mountain Trail in the saddle between Secret Mountain and the Mogollon Rim. Turn left here and climb the short distance to the rim and the Secret Mountain Trailhead. Views are limited here, but if you walk a few hundred yards along the road, there is a great view down Loy Canyon.

21
DOE MOUNTAIN

Description: The top of Doe Mountain features fine views of Bear Mountain and the Dry Creek basin.
Location: 6.0 miles northwest of Sedona.
Type of trail: Trail and cross-country loop.
Difficulty: Easy.
Total distance: 2.8 miles.
High point: 5,540 feet.
Elevation change: 440 feet.
Time required: 2 hours.
Water: None.
Best season: All year.
Maps: Wilson Mountain USGS quad; Coconino National Forest.
Permits and restrictions: A Red Rock Pass is required for vehicle parking.
For more information: Sedona Ranger District, Coconino National Forest; (928) 282–4119.

Finding the trailhead: From Sedona drive to the west end of town on Arizona 89A, and then turn right at a traffic light onto Dry Creek Road. Drive 2.8 miles, and then turn left onto Boynton Canyon Road. Continue 1.6 miles, and then turn left onto Forest Road 152C, a maintained dirt road. Go 1.3 miles to the Bear Mountain Trailhead, which is on the right.

Doe Mountain, Fay Canyon Arch, Boynton Canyon, Long Canyon

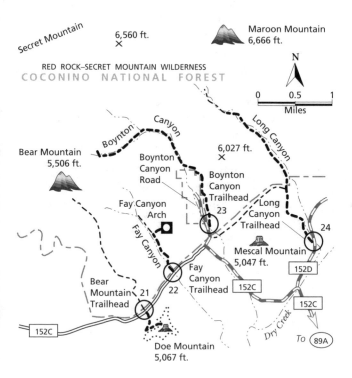

Secret Mountain

6,560 ft.
×

Maroon Mountain
6,666 ft.

RED ROCK–SECRET MOUNTAIN WILDERNESS
COCONINO NATIONAL FOREST

N

0   0.5   1
Miles

Boynton Canyon

Long Canyon

Bear Mountain
5,506 ft.

Boynton
Canyon
Road

6,027 ft.
×

Boynton
Canyon
Trailhead

23

Fay Canyon
Arch

Fay Canyon

Long
Canyon
Trailhead

24

Mescal Mountain
5,047 ft.

152D

Bear
Mountain
Trailhead

21

22

Fay
Canyon
Trailhead

152C

152C

152C

Dry Creek

To 89A

Doe Mountain
5,067 ft.

Key points:
0.0 Bear Mountain Trailhead.
0.5 Doe Mountain rim.
2.3 Doe Mountain Trail.
2.8 Bear Mountain Trailhead.

The hike: Doe Mountain is the flat, red mesa to the southwest. Cross the road and walk up the Doe Mountain Trail, which starts by heading directly toward a large ravine that splits the northwest side of the mesa. After a few hundred yards, the trail turns right as the slope becomes steeper. A single, long switchback takes the trail back into the ravine, which it climbs to reach the rim of Doe Mountain. The trail ends, but now turn right and follow the rim cross-country all the way around the top of Doe Mountain. The walk is easy and nearly level, and your reward is a series of views in all directions. Rejoin the trail to return to the trailhead.

22
FAY CANYON ARCH

see map page 67

Description: A hike to a natural arch in the Red Rock–Secret Mountain Wilderness.
Location: 5.0 miles northwest of Sedona.
Type of trail: Out-and-back.
Difficulty: Easy.
Total distance: 1.6 miles.
High point: 5,110 feet.
Elevation change: 220 feet.
Time required: 1 hour.
Water: None.
Best season: All year.
Maps: Wilson Mountain USGS quad; Coconino National Forest.
Permits and restrictions: A Red Rock Pass is required for vehicle parking.
For more information: Sedona Ranger District, Coconino National Forest; (928) 282–4119.

Finding the trailhead: From Sedona drive to the west end of town on Arizona 89A, and then turn right at a traffic light onto Dry Creek Road. Drive 2.8 miles, and then turn left onto Boynton Canyon Road. Continue 1.6 miles, and then turn left onto Forest Road 152C, a maintained dirt road. Go 0.5 mile to the Fay Canyon Trailhead, which is on the right.

Key points:
0.0 Fay Canyon Trailhead.
0.6 Arch turnoff.
0.8 Fay Canyon Arch.

The hike: The Fay Canyon Trail starts out as an easy walk through pinyon-juniper forest. The only difficulty is a few false trails near the beginning. About 0.6 mile from the trailhead, watch for an unmarked trail going right (northeast) toward the canyon wall. This trail climbs steeply about 0.2 mile to Fay Canyon Arch, which is difficult to see until you are very close. The arch was formed from a massive fin in the Schnebly Hill formation and stands close to the cliff behind it, so there is little skylight shining through.

It is also worthwhile to continue on the main trail up Fay Canyon. It fades out at a fork in the canyon about 1.0 mile from the trailhead; this side trip would add 0.8 mile to the hike.

23
BOYNTON CANYON

see map page 67

Description: This is a very popular hike into a spectacular red-rock canyon that ends below the towering cliffs of Bear Mountain in the Red Rock–Secret Mountain Wilderness.

Location: 5.0 miles northwest of Sedona.

Type of trail: Out-and-back.

Difficulty: Easy.

Total distance: 5.0 miles.

High point: 5,200 feet.

Elevation change: 540 feet.

Time required: 3 hours.

Water: None.

Best season: All year.

Maps: Wilson Mountain USGS quad; Coconino National Forest.

Permits and restrictions: A Red Rock Pass is required for vehicle parking.

For more information: Sedona Ranger District, Coconino National Forest; (928) 282–4119.

Finding the trailhead: From Sedona drive to the west end of town on Arizona 89A, and then turn right at the traffic light onto Dry Creek Road. Continue 2.8 miles, and then turn left onto Boynton Canyon Road. Drive 1.6 miles, and then turn right, remaining on Boynton Canyon Road. Go

0.3 mile and park at the Boynton Canyon Trailhead on the right. (The road continues into a private resort.)

Key points:
0.0 Boynton Trailhead.
1.0 Spur trail to the resort.
2.5 End of the trail below Bear Mountain.

The hike: This is a well-known hike that skirts a large resort for its first mile, so don't expect a wilderness experience. The upper part of Boynton Canyon is spectacular and makes up for the initial section of the hike.

The Boynton Canyon Trail climbs along the north side of the canyon to avoid the resort and then drops into the canyon. Here a spur trail to the resort joins from the left. The Boynton Canyon Trail follows the drainage to the northwest. In another 0.5 mile or so, both the canyon and the trail turn toward the southwest, and the noises of the resort are left behind. The head of the canyon is formed by massive walls of Coconino sandstone on the east face of Bear Mountain. The trail becomes fainter near the end as it winds through cool pine and fir forest. A final short climb leads out of the dense forest to a view-point on the brushy slope above. Allow some time to linger at this fine spot.

24

LONG CANYON

see map page 67

Description: An easy hike to a less-visited canyon in the Red Rock–Secret Mountain Wilderness.

Location: 5.0 miles northwest of Sedona.

Type of trail: Out-and-back.

Difficulty: Easy.

Total distance: 4.8 miles.

High point: 5,200 feet.

Elevation change: 320 feet.

Time required: 3 hours.

Water: None.

Best season: All year.

Maps: Wilson Mountain USGS quad; Coconino National Forest.

Permits and restrictions: A Red Rock Pass is required for vehicle parking.

For more information: Sedona Ranger District, Coconino National Forest; (928) 282–4119.

Finding the trailhead: From Sedona drive to the west end of town on Arizona 89A, and then turn right at the traffic light onto the Dry Creek Road, Forest Road 152C. Continue 2.8 miles, and then turn right onto Long Canyon Road, Forest Road 152D. Drive 0.6 mile to the trailhead parking on the left. (The road continues to a private subdivision.)

Key points:
0.0 Long Canyon Trailhead.
1.0 Deadman Pass Trail.
2.4 End of trail.

The hike: The mouth of Long Canyon is more than a mile from the trailhead, so the first portion of the hike is through open pinyon-juniper flats. This pleasant section of the trail offers tantalizing views of the canyon walls ahead, as well as Mescal Mountain to the south. As you pass the north tip of Mescal Mountain, you'll reach the wilderness boundary and the junction with the Deadman Pass Trail.

The canyon walls gradually close in as you continue, and the trail starts to fade out. It's possible to continue the hike cross-country and also to explore several side canyons. If you end the hike when the trail fades out, you'll be turning back about 2.4 miles from the trailhead.

25
DEVILS BRIDGE

Description: A short hike to a striking natural arch in the Red Rock–Secret Mountain Wilderness.

Location: 3.0 miles northeast of Sedona.

Type of trail: Out-and-back.

Difficulty: Easy.

Total distance: 1.4 miles.

High point: 4,900 feet.

Elevation change: 300 feet.

Time required: 1 hour.

Water: None.

Best season: All year.

Maps: Wilson Mountain USGS quad; Coconino National Forest.

Permits and restrictions: A Red Rock Pass is required for vehicle parking.

For more information: Sedona Ranger District, Coconino National Forest; (928) 282–4119.

Finding the trailhead: From Sedona drive to the west end of town on Arizona 89A, and then turn right at a traffic light onto Dry Creek Road. After 2.0 miles turn right on dirt Forest Road 152 (also called Dry Creek Road). Although this road is maintained, it receives heavy traffic, and its condition varies. Drive 1.2 miles, and then turn right into

Devils Bridge

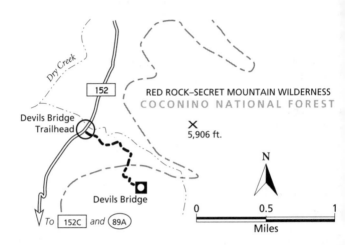

the Devils Bridge Trailhead. Parking is limited, but there are other parking spots nearby.

Key points:
0.0 Trailhead.
0.4 Trail turns uphill.
0.7 Devils Bridge.

The hike: On the first section of the walk, you'll parallel a wash. The trail is well used and easy to follow. Then the trail turns right and starts to climb the slope toward the imposing mass of Capitol Butte. It soon reaches a red sandstone ledge and works its way to the top via a series of stone steps. Follow the trail a few hundred feet east to the top of the bridge.

Devils Bridge is actually a natural arch, since it doesn't span a stream course. The arch was formed by weathering of both sides of the narrow sandstone fir. First, water erosion exploited a joint, or crack, in the rock that was parallel to the rim, eventually separating the fin from the main ledge. Then, weathering of the natural cement holding the sand grains together caused the base of the fin to grow thinner. Finally, the fin was eroded completely through, and the arch was formed.

Several natural features in the Sedona area bear names starting with devil. The common explanation is that the early settlers found travel through the area so difficult before good trails and roads were built that they referred to the Sedona area as "Hells Hole."

26
BRINS MESA TRAIL

Description: This hike leads to a very scenic viewpoint overlooking Sedona, Dry Creek, and the high cliffs of Wilson Mountain. It is in the Red Rock–Secret Mountain Wilderness.

Location: 4.0 miles northwest of Sedona.

Type of trail: Out-and-back.

Difficulty: Easy.

Total distance: 4.8 miles.

High point: 5,120 feet.

Elevation change: 500 feet.

Time required: 3 hours.

Water: None.

Best season: All year.

Maps: Wilson Mountain USGS quad; Coconino National Forest.

Permits and restrictions: A Red Rock Pass is required for vehicle parking.

For more information: Sedona Ranger District, Coconino National Forest; (928) 282–4119.

Finding the trailhead: From Sedona drive to the west end of town on Arizona 89A, and then turn right at a traffic light onto Dry Creek Road. After 2.0 miles turn right on dirt Forest Road 152 (also called Dry Creek Road). Although this road is maintained, it receives a great deal of traffic,

Brins Mesa Trail

and its condition varies. Drive 2.2 miles, and then turn right into the trailhead parking area. Parking is limited, but there are other parking spots nearby.

Key points:
0.0 Trailhead.
1.1 Soldier Pass Trail; stay left.
2.4 Brins Mesa and viewpoint.

The hike: A small metal sign at the east side of the parking area marks the start of the Brins Mesa Trail. About 1.1

miles from the trailhead, the unsigned Soldier Pass Trail turns right (south). Stay left, on the Brins Mesa Trail. For nearly 2.0 miles the trail follows a normally dry wash, crossing the bed as necessary. The forest is mixed pinyon pine, juniper, and Arizona cypress, and views are limited until the trail climbs onto Brins Mesa. After crossing the flat mesa, the trail drops abruptly off the southeast rim. This scenic spot is the goal for your hike.

You're standing on the Schnebly Hill formation, which is responsible for most of the red sandstone cliffs and rock formations in the Sedona area. It was deposited in a coastal tidal-flat environment, and repeated exposure to the air oxidized traces of iron in the rock to create the red color. The buff-colored cliffs above you to the east, forming the impressive west face of Wilson Mountain, are Coconino sandstone. This thick layer of rock was originally deposited in a dry, sand-dune desert, much like the modern Sahara. Gray layers of volcanic basalt rocks laid down in lava flows cap the rim of Wilson Mountain. The hard basalt protects the softer rocks below, so that erosion by water has shaped Wilson Mountain into a flat topped mesa. In contrast look southwest at Capitol Butte. It lacks a basalt cap to protect it, and the soft Coconino sandstone has eroded into a dome shape.

27
SECRET CANYON

Description: This is an exceptionally fine hike up the longest canyon in the Red Rock–Secret Mountain Wilderness. Its length keeps the crowds away.

Location: 5.0 miles northwest of Sedona.

Type of trail: Out-and-back.

Difficulty: Moderate.

Total distance: 7.8 miles.

High point: 5,150 feet.

Elevation change: 480 feet.

Time required: 5 hours.

Water: Upper Secret Canyon.

Best season: All year.

Maps: Wilson Mountain USGS quad; Coconino National Forest.

Permits and restrictions: A Red Rock Pass is required for vehicle parking.

For more information: Sedona Ranger District, Coconino National Forest; (928) 282–4119.

Finding the trailhead: From Sedona drive to the west end of town on Arizona 89A, and then turn right at a traffic light onto Dry Creek Road. After 2.0 miles turn right on dirt Forest Road 152 (also called Dry Creek Road). Although this road is maintained, it receives heavy traffic, and its condition varies. Drive 3.2 miles to the Secret Canyon

Secret Canyon, Dry Creek, Bear Sign Canyon, Vultee Arch

Trailhead on the left side of the road. The parking area is small, but there are other parking spots nearby.

Key points:
0.0 Secret Canyon Trailhead.
1.8 Small clearing.
3.9 End of trail in Secret Canyon.

The hike: Secret Canyon is the longest and most remote canyon in the Dry Creek basin, and it is nearly as long as its more famous neighbor, Oak Creek. It also has a permanent stream in the upper section, a rarity in the redrock area.

The Secret Canyon Trail crosses Dry Creek and enters the Red Rock–Secret Mountain Wilderness only a few yards from the road. You'll cross Secret Canyon wash several times; if either it or Dry Creek are flooding, this hike will be impossible. Normally, however, lower Secret Canyon is dry, and the hike is easy through the pinyon-juniper-cypress forest. About 0.5 mile from the trailhead, the HS Canyon Trail branches left. Just before the trail enters upper Secret Canyon, it passes through a small clearing that gives you good views. The trail contours along the north side of the drainage for a short distance before dropping back into the bed. The canyon walls, which are formed by the Mogollon Rim on the north and Maroon Mountain on the south, become narrower here. There is normally water in this section. Watch for poison ivy, a low-growing plant with shiny leaves that grow in groups of three. Fall colors in this part of the canyon are a beautiful mix of reds, oranges, and violets, with most of the color provided by Arizona big-tooth maples and poison ivy. About 3.9 miles from the trailhead, our hike ends as the trail fades out.

28
DRY CREEK

see map page 82

Description: This is an easy hike into the headwaters of Dry Creek, in the Red Rock–Secret Mountain Wilderness.
Location: 6.0 miles northwest of Sedona.
Type of trip: Out-and-back.
Difficulty: Easy.
Total distance: 2.2 miles.
Elevation change: 260 feet.
High point: 5,040 feet.
Time required: 2 hours.
Water: Seasonal in Dry Creek.
Best season: All year.
Maps: Wilson Mountain USGS quad; Coconino National Forest.
Permits and restrictions: A Red Rock Pass is required for vehicle parking.
For more information: Sedona Ranger District, Coconino National Forest; (928) 282–4119.

Finding the trailhead: From Sedona drive to the west end of town on Arizona 89A, and then turn right at a traffic light onto Dry Creek Road. After 2.0 miles turn right on dirt Forest Road 152 (also called Dry Creek Road). Although this road is maintained, it receives heavy traffic, and its condition varies. Drive 4.0 miles to the end of the road at the Dry Creek Trailhead.

Key points:
0.0 Dry Creek Trailhead.
0.6 Bear Sign Canyon Trail.
1.1 Trail fades out.

The hike: Follow the Dry Creek Trail north out of the parking area. After 0.6 mile Bear Sign Canyon branches left; stay right on the trail along Dry Creek. The informal trail becomes fainter as you proceed farther from the trailhead and fades out completely after about 1.1 miles. This makes a good destination for an easy day hike. Ahead, to the north, Dry Creek becomes a steep, rough canyon, as it heads under the Mogollon Rim. The striking point towering above you to the east is East Pocket, a promontory on the Mogollon Rim. Some of the early settlers used the term "pocket" to refer to an isolated section of land, generally surrounded by cliffs on three sides and only accessible from the fourth. In this case no pioneer trail was ever built to East Pocket from Dry Creek.

Sedona and the Red Rock Country lies under the western portion of the Mogollon Rim. This 200-mile-long, south-facing escarpment starts just west of Sedona and runs east–southeast across Arizona before merging with the Mogollon Mountains in New Mexico. The south-facing slopes and cliffs are up to 2,000 feet high, and the rim forms an unmistakable natural boundary between the lofty plateaus and deep canyons of the Colorado Plateau to the north and the rugged mountains of central Arizona to the south.

29
BEAR SIGN CANYON

see map page 82

Description: A very easy hike into a red-rock canyon in the Red Rock–Secret Mountain Wilderness.
Location: 6.0 miles northwest of Sedona.
Type of trail: Out-and-back.
Difficulty: Easy.
Total distance: 3.2 miles.
High point: 5,080 feet.
Elevation change: 280 feet.
Time required: 2 hours.
Water: Seasonal in Bear Sign Canyon.
Best season: All year.
Maps: Wilson Mountain USGS quad; Coconino National Forest.
Permits and restrictions: A Red Rock Pass is required for vehicle parking.
For more information: Sedona Ranger District, Coconino National Forest; (928) 282–4119.

Finding the trailhead: From Sedona drive to the west end of town on Arizona 89A, and then turn right at a traffic light onto Dry Creek Road. After 2.0 miles turn right on dirt Forest Road 152 (also called Dry Creek Road). Although this road is maintained, it receives heavy traffic, and its condition varies. Drive 4.0 miles to the end of the road at the Dry Creek Trailhead.

Key points:
0.0 Dry Creek Trailhead.
0.6 Turn left onto Bear Sign Canyon Trail.
1.6 End of the hike as the trail fades out.

The hike: Start out on the Dry Creek Trail. (There are two trails that begin at this trailhead. The Dry Creek Trail goes north, and the Vultee Arch Trail goes east.) Hike 0.6 mile north, and then turn left (northwest) at Bear Sign Canyon, the first side canyon on the left. The trail continues about a mile up Bear Sign Canyon before fading out. It is possible to go farther, but the canyon becomes much rougher. There are great views of the cliffs of the Mogollon Rim, and after wet periods the creek will be running. The vegetation is the usual, but still delightful, mix of Arizona cypress, pinyon pine, juniper trees, and chaparral brush.

30
VULTEE ARCH

see map page 82

Description: A pleasant walk to a graceful natural arch in the Red Rock–Secret Mountain Wilderness.

Location: 6.0 miles northwest of Sedona.

Type of trail: Out-and-back.

Difficulty: Easy.

Total distance: 3.6 miles.

High point: 5,500 feet.

Elevation change: 600 feet.

Time required: 2.5 hours.

Water: None.

Best season: All year.

Maps: Wilson Mountain USGS quad; Coconino National Forest.

Permits and restrictions: A Red Rock Pass is required for vehicle parking.

For more information: Sedona Ranger District, Coconino National Forest; (928) 282–4119.

Finding the trailhead: From Sedona drive to the west end of town on Arizona 89A, and then turn right at a traffic light onto Dry Creek Road. After 2.0 miles turn right on dirt Forest Road 152 (also called Dry Creek Road). Although this road is maintained, it receives heavy traffic, and its condition varies. Drive 4.0 miles to the end of the road at the Dry Creek Trailhead.

Key points:
1.0 Dry Creek Trailhead.
1.8 Vultee Arch.

The hike: Hike east on the Vultee Arch Trail, which follows Sterling Canyon. This is an easy walk through pleasant pinyon-juniper-cypress forest, and the canyon is nearly straight. After about 1.6 miles, right where Sterling Canyon takes a turn to the southeast, follow an unsigned trail left (north) out of the bed to reach the arch. It was named after the president of Vultee Aircraft who was killed in a plane crash nearby in the 1930s.

About the Author

Bruce Grubbs is an avid hiker, climber, mountain biker, and cross-country skier who has been exploring the American West for more than 30 years. An outdoor writer and photographer, he has written thirteen other FalconGuides. He lives in Flagstaff, Arizona.